Relationships:
A Survival Guide

Professor Barry A. Goodfield, Ph.D.,
DABFM

CONTENTS

Dedication

For Dori
Forever Now Forever

To my teachers past and present, you know who you are ... Thank you!

Barry

Preface

I am Wim de Leeuw, a Presbyterian Minister, biblical scholar, theologian, Senior Goodfield Therapist and Goodfield Non-Verbal Strategy Analyst.

What's more, I am the guy who walked into the practice of Dr. Barry Goodfield and uttered the infamous words, "I am here because I am having a *relationshit* problem." My true unconscious thought came out as I came in.

Barry and I have forged a life long friendship. We changed many lives, including our own.

This book, *Relationships: A Survival Guide*, gives me a platform to say a few words about him as well as the book.

What he says about being in the "here and now" and living in the present is actually a correct reading of the first chapter of the Bible, where time and space are cut down to human size. We have the opportunity to really live life and we have as many lives as we have days.

This belief is at the core of Barry's belief both personally and professionally. He is a true lover of life who believes in people as much as he believes in change itself.

S.I. Hayakawa his mentor, said of him once, "Goodfield has the faith of a General Semanticist, namely that where people are present change is possible."

I must say, reflecting on the Goodfield workshops, I have forgiveness and even appreciation in my heart when on some occasions the air in the workshop would turn "blue" with blasphemous words and remarks that took the name of the Lord in vain. That was all right with me because the people who did it were working hard and honestly to get rid of their pain and anger. I have seen some of the most beautiful things of my life there: real humanity, forgiveness, mercy, laughter and tears, swearing, love, fun and what not.

Faith is one thing, reading the unconscious messages that show in our Non-Verbal Leaks, as he calls them, is quite another.

That hidden world has become his life's stomping ground. After years of probing with intuition and later scientific tools, he received two U.S. Patents as beliefs became proof. He was also an early pioneer (if not the first) to combine video with therapy.

During my three decades with Barry and his staff, I watched and assisted as people grew and renewed their relationships using a foundation of honesty and directness. This book, *Relationships: A Survival Guide*, is filled with little cartoon characters he calls "Real's." They present the insights into the fundamentals of a great relationship. Over the years I have found these little people written on my walls, napkins and other strange locations. In this book he has found a few of these little friends to help him make his point even more clear.

Throughout the book, life's truths regarding relationships are presented in a thought-provoking, yet simple way.

So here's to life and its marvelous opportunities. If there is one commandment that sticks out above the ten "ordinary" ones, it is; *Thou shall L I V E*!! And if that is true, as I know it to be, you better live it as if each day is your last one, which it may very well be.

And may *Relationships: A Survival Guide* help you to have even more quality in your life with your significant others, your friends and loved ones - for we all know that mankind is not meant to be alone and life must be lived together, or it does not deserve that name.

Amen, so be it and may you never have a Bad Relationshit ever again!

Wim de Leeuw

Eindhoven, The Netherlands

Introduction

This book is a mosaic made not of tiles or stone, but of people and places. The design and shape ultimately are about my experiences and lessons learned.

Throughout life we are influenced by and affected by the individuals and events around us. My mosaic in that sense is no different than anyone else's.

The following pages take the wisdom that I have abstracted from others, and internalized into my own approach to life. As a psychotherapist for many years, I have learned the lessons taught to me by so many who sought and received help while, at the same time, they taught me some of the fundamental principles of what works and does not work for the individuals and their relationships.

One thing is sure; the truth is a matter of perception. It is around these translations of our world that our Weltanschauung or "Life view" emerges into who we are, who we become.

Relationships: A Survival Guide is the product of my personal mosaic.

In this book you will find cartoons of my little friends I call "Reals" - Characters that leaked out of my unconscious many years ago; they always deal with *real-life* situations.

They remained unnamed for years until, one day a pal of mine, Mort Rosenblum, inadvertently changed all that. He was getting dressed and, as I waited for him, I noticed, on the top of his dresser, his wallet lying open. There were engraved words in gold saying "Real Leather."

I thought: "What a terrible thing to do to a "Real!" At that moment I knew the name of the "little leaks" that had remained nameless for oh, so many years.

Relationships: A Survival Guide is designed to give you a real opportunity to think about the way you think. To reflect on the basic assumptions upon which you have built your life. It gives practical suggestions regarding your relationships. Some of these insights, although true, were not as funny as I learned the lessons.

The real truth is that you have only *today*. Have a real remarkable time with my little friends and the REAL truth they try to illustrate.

Of course, I hope these insights lead to REAL fun and genuine happiness in your life!

I hope you enjoy it, will learn from it. I especially hope the GIVE test at the end of the book will mark a new beginning for you - and your relationships.

Trust the process,

Barry

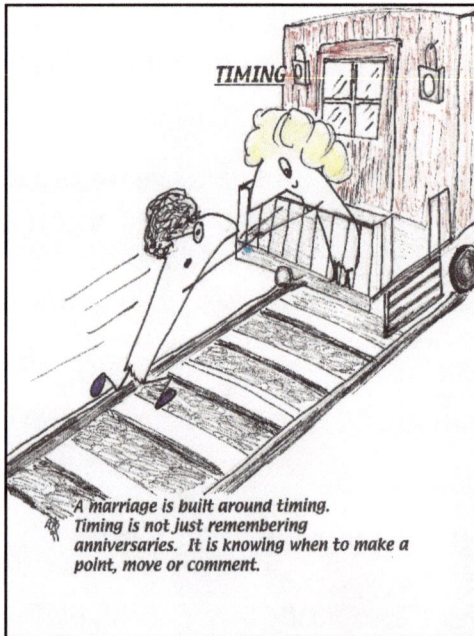

A marriage is built around timing. Timing is not just remembering anniversaries. It is knowing when to make a point, move or comment.

Chapter 1:

THE NECESSARY PREREQUISITES TO A GOOD RELATIONSHIP

Before you begin delving into this book, let's look at a few prerequisites for a quality relationship.

Respect and love for one's self

Love for another is in direct proportion to the degree to which you love yourself. It is syllogistic and fallacious logic to believe, that in a relationship, two halves make a whole. Many relationships are destined to fail, when they are entered in an attempt to compensate, for what is lacking within one's self.

I believe this fact alone can contribute to a deeper understanding of the soaring divorce rate. Unfortunately, these insights relating to this fact are usually gleaned on a post hoc basis, after the many tears have been shed and the relationship has failed.

The remark, *"Know Thyself"* in that sense, isn't just "graffiti" written on the walls of the Temple of Apollo in Delphi in the 4th century B.C.

An understanding of your own family culture

Context determines meaning and perception determines reality. We are a "symbolic" class of life and the symbols and trappings from our past; help us to understand what is right and meaningful for us now.

Our early family programming becomes a benchmark. A kind of guide, that helps us understand the meaning and motives of what we're doing. It also helps us to understand why were doing it, and how successful we are in our endeavors. When we begin the process of selecting a mate or partner, the role of our family and the programming we received during our upbringing, becomes important on both conscious and unconscious levels.

Mannerisms, personal preferences, and style become increasingly important as the relationship progresses.

The classic lament to the "crime" of leaving the top off of the toothpaste, or worse, leaving the top up on the toilet seat after you left the bathroom, is a reflection of our old programming and a new problem, on the horizon. In most cases these are never the issues at the beginning of a relationship. They can become a symbolic explanation about differences experienced in the relationship over time.

An understanding of your daily needs and lifestyle

One of the keys to success in a relationship is the ability to compromise. Or as Kenny Rogers says in his song the Gambler, *"It's knowing when to hold them and knowing when to fold them."*

Compromise and flexibility go hand-in-hand in any successful relationship. It is the notion of goodwill, fairness and, giving the other person in the relationship, the benefit of the doubt. Anybody considering entering a serious relationship, had better be able to put a check by this box!

An understanding of your expectations now and in the future

This is another important consideration. This has practical, psychological, and philosophical considerations that must be clear if you are going to win the coin flip regarding divorce statistics.

Before misunderstanding turns to mayhem, it is important to be clear about what your personal expectations are in a relationship. I would even suggest, that it would be smart to take a pen and paper and list your expectations on all three levels. (The GIVE test at the end of this book can be very helpful here).

Be mentally healthy; marry mentally healthy

In all my years of living and learning, I think this is perhaps one of the most important things that I know about successful relationships.

At the risk of sounding utopian or naïve, I believe it is important to acknowledge the role of mental health here. As you will see in the book, the role of perception is emphasized as a key factor in a successful contact within a relationship. I think it's safe to say, that some of the craziest people saw themselves as the most mentally healthy.

4

If people are capable of getting beyond the initial self-delusion that goes with the first blush of relationship where excitement, expectation and desire filter, and inhibit good judgment, then the most important consideration is the stability of the potential partner.

As a guy who collects antique automobiles, I know that most of the time you may find the right model and make. Maybe it will require work to bring it to its original standard of excellence. And so it is with the relationship. You follow somebody and s/he may need some work. This is not to say that you couldn't stand the tune-up as well.

When this is the case, honesty and openness are the most important things in the toolbox to fix the relationship. Here's where counseling, individual or collective therapy and a willingness to address individual and collective issues, can be so important.

The restoration process doesn't necessarily have to be painful or difficult. Keep in mind the goal and the mutual desire to find balance and happiness.

Some years ago there was a popular remark allegedly attributed to Albert Einstein that said: "*Men marry women with the hope that they will never change. Women marry men with the hope they will change. Invariably they are both disappointed.*"

The kind of mentality that says, "I won't worry about it now; I'll fix it later," has put many cars stuck along the roadside and, many relationships in the ditch!

It's more important to find somebody with a beautiful interior than a beautiful exterior. It is even better when you find both, but what is under the hood is more important than how shiny the paint job is.

There is absolutely no chance that I am wrong about this, none whatsoever!

Attempted repairs done on pre-existing conditions generate resentment, frustration, and all the other things that lead to catastrophe in a couple.

Buyers beware!

Communication

It would be remiss of me, as a former protégé of Dr. S. I. Hayakawa and Dr. Bill. Pemberton, two of the foremost experts in the world on communication and General Semantics, not to mention the role of communication in general when it comes to interpersonal relationships.

We as people are basically human bio-computers when it comes to programming. The adage of "garbage in and garbage out" often abbreviated as GIGO applies to us, as well as the fancy computers we have.

The garbage in the human bio- computer begins with false assumptions, personal bias and a closed mind, that sees other minds as close as they do not agree with theirs.

Rather than going into a long dissertation about the conscious and unconscious aspects of the communication process let me simply say this. What we bring in terms of assumptions and fundamental beliefs, will ultimately determine our success and failure in our interactions with others.

An important book to look at is written by S. I. Hayakawa entitled, _Language in Thought and Action._ In this book basic principles of communication are discussed, with practical discussions for improvement. I can also suggest that you read my book _Insight and Action_.

KEYS TO A GREAT RELATIONSHIP

Chapter 2:

WHAT IS THE PRICE OF PERSONAL BALANCE?

I would like to review the price tag we all pay for our daily existence.

It is quite clear that all people have a position values and strategies regarding tools to make it through life on a daily basis. I will simply review the basics, as I understand them, so we may consider the price tag we pay each day to survive life's challenges.

Perhaps we might even find a "better way" of doing things?

Here is a list of things to do every day, which I feel, will help provide two important essentials. They're designed to help keep you focused on the here and now, and to provide a greater perspective of the price tags paid to live the intense life that is required to be successful.

In essence the question is one of balance. What do I need to do daily to find and maintain a healthy balance between work, family and personal objectives?

Needless to say, this question can be looked at regarding many people's daily struggle to find harmony in a busy lifestyle. The list of ten items that are in the essence of thousands of people's conclusions and years of laments and regrets that usually contained the message of "if only I had," or "I wish I had known," or "things would be different now if I had done that."

Let me paraphrase a comment attributed to the late U.S. Sen. Paul Tsongas who suffered and died from lymphoma. "No one on his deathbed ever says I wish I had spent more time on my business." I said: "A few people say I wish I had spent more time on my business." The message is the same. Be here and now, live here and now, enjoy here and now that's all we have got.

In a relationship, a marriage or a partnership, like any other interaction that involves people, there are rules. Like any game or sport, it has a beginning, middle, and an end. There are a dozen or so rules that govern a play at all points of the game. What is clear is that no marriage or relationship can be called successful unless everybody is willing to give. It is give as in give-and-take or compromise. It is give as in sharing ideas, feelings, and quality time.

Sometimes, giving is done with magnanimity, other times, it is a simple *quid pro quo* arrangement. No matter how you cut it, quality relationships require an investment of time and serious involvement, before the real fun of a true relationship can blossom and grow.

Whether in business, in bed, or both, the partners' openness is one of the main keys to success in any relationship. Risk-taking is in direct proportion to growth. It can also be said, that risk-taking is in direct proportion to failure.

The human being is a funny creature. We strive for balance. When we find it we look for another challenge, personally or professionally, that puts the previously established balance in jeopardy. This has to do with our definition of ourselves or, what we call in psychology, our self-concept.

Personal balance is a key component in any game. Enclosed you will find 10 ways how to keep your personal balance. A worksheet is provided to explore these issues and ideas.

Like other games of chance or skill, it is best not to change the rules during play.

In some games it is considered fair and, even necessary, to grab the ball and run. Some sports allow players to be changed, swooped or traded to improve a team's chance.

In the marriage game, like most other games, players start as amateurs. Unlike other games however, the more times you play, the less likely you are to really be successful. Practice doesn't make perfect, any more than marry early, and marry often builds relationship skills.

As in the game of tennis, love is sometimes mentioned when evaluating the score, but it is not what wins the game.

Victory, unlike most any other sport, is only achieved when both parties win. In fact the highest score is achieved when, after many, many years, one player dies while still in play.

To some the relationship game seems too rough to even consider playing. Frequently telling stories of physical and emotional pain puts off some, while potential economic losses suffered at the end of play dissuade others.

A relationship is somewhat like a horse race, you must try to stay in the saddle, keep on track, use the whip sparingly, don't waste your time looking back and hope your horse does not turn out to be a nag.

Some sports allow bringing other players into the game. Data on the 'sport' of marriage suggests that the original two starters should play alone. Adding a participant, while often tempting, can severely alter the play and may be very costly in the end.

Ultimately the rules for success in the game are simple: Be a good sport, try to play fair, know your limitations, learn the rules and enjoy yourself.

Following are a number of very practical tips I picked up along the way.

Let's look at some basic principles that are tied up in one way or another with all successes and all failures in a relationship. As you may know by now, I have a Ph.D. in psychology. I have gone through a dozen years of whoops and hollers listening, writing and passing tests.

Most anybody, with real tenacity and an obsession to not be beaten by rules and regulations, can become an academically "certified expert" in human behavior. What I am sharing with you now did not pop out of a book or a professor's mouth. It came from my life experience and the lessons I have learned from thousands of people in my clinical practice, who trusted me to help them search for and achieve a greater understanding of themselves.

I learned much of this also on the street, sometimes the Boulevard of Broken Dreams.

In order to share some of the rules of my relationship knowledge, I feel it would be useful to share my own life and experiences.

First, let me say that I am an 'expert' in this area. I spent more than one half of a century in a relationship with one person or another. Some failed for one reason or another. Why?

I will share with you the secrets to my more outstanding catastrophes detailed in principle only, so that those who were willing to mate with me, mingle with me and even marry me are spared the embarrassment of exposure.

12

Chapter 3:

KEYS TO A BETTER PERSONAL BALACE

Here's what I have been taught and continue to learn in my 40+ years of clinical practice.

1. Clear boundary setting
(What I will and will not do)

Perhaps the biggest contributor to stress and family breakdown is failure to set clear boundaries. When pressed to overextend or simply disregard personal boundaries, it is only a matter of time before there will be some sort of system failure. Of this, there is no doubt. You know what will happen when you block one of the basic systems in the body. There will be increased pressure, followed by system breakdown and then death. What makes you think intra-psychic, psychophysical and interpersonal systems are different in any other way? They are not, is the short answer.

Perhaps the good news about you is also the bad news in the long run. Your power and focus can become the basis for your own system break down. For many people, their need to be strong is their greatest weakness.

Know this, you may verbally and consciously say yes to overstepping your boundaries or letting others do so, but it will come back on you one way or another in the end, you can count on this fact.

2. *Be here and now*
(With all the good and bad news that implies)

It is important to be in the moment. How much of the intensity and pressure do you bring home from work?

How much of "there and then" generally permeates your personal life in the "here and now". Lack of participation with equally important issues at home can wreck a marriage and derail your happiness into a psychological ditch.

3. *Trust your feelings*
(Accept them over others' reality)

Your feelings are never wrong, but our perceptions often are. When we get married to our misperceptions, we often become divorced from reality. Check with your family for feedback on this one.

The point is simple; when you experience any feeling it is because your perceptual field tells you that this is the reality. The reaction to that perception should always be tempered with the awareness that it is simply one person's reality and not "the truth from on high".

For some people this is a hard lesson to learn. The day is full of hours of thinking and acting on the "truth" you see it through your own eyes. One misperception, one moment of self-doubt at the wrong time, can mean it's game over for someone. If everyone's perceived reality was "right" all the time, pencils would come without erasers. We still need that little rubber thing. Walt Whitman said it well in his poem *Leaves Of Grass*: "You shall listen to all sides, and filter them from yourself."

4. *Be able and willing to make contact*
(And in your own way)

Regardless of how you put it, we all need and want contact.
For some people contact is superficial. While for others it must be deep and profound. The determining factor is the programming of our human bio-computer. Early experiences teach us the value and safety associated with this basic human need.

If our initial contact with our mother and father was problematic, then we learn to defend ourselves from the perceived danger associated with contact. Even as we protect ourselves from contact we still long for it. Sometimes we seek it out in short-term, intense, superficial relationships. This strategy ends up often generating more heat than light. Although others may look on with envy, when practiced for any length of time, loneliness festers inside like a progressive, insidious disease.

Genuine contact requires more of an investment than gaining a formal education. Although real contact is deep, it is as simple as a glance from a child. Make a commitment to have it in your life or pay the price of not having it.

> "All truths wait in all things,
> They neither hasten their own delivery nor resist it,

> They do not need the obstetric forceps of the surgeon,
> The insignificant is as big to me as any,
> (What is less or more than a touch)..."

Walt Whitman, _Leaves Of Grass._ (1855)

I think he had it right, "What is more than a touch?"

5. Say what you feel
(Value being clear over being liked)

Sometimes we say things that are untrue because it is expedient or simply easier. This strategy can become a type of insulation from contact and pressure but there is a price tag in this approach to others.

My speculation is that many people do not see themselves as the "warm and fuzzy" type. For the most part they see themselves as skilled professionals with a particular viewpoint as a basis for their daily actions.

The hard truth is no problem, facts are facts. Right? It is not the hard truth that is hard, it is the emotional truths that are sometimes perceived as insurmountable.

Talking about deeper feelings is often the big challenge for many people as you know. Learning how to do so, and making it a priority, will not necessarily make life easier but it will add more depth and, hence, more meaning.

6. Be open to difference
(Hear things that may be hard to hear, listen while keeping your mouth shut and your ears open)

This is perhaps one of the most difficult things to do for bright and logical people. The ultimate testing ground is children and the ones at home who see you as someone who does not understand or see you as an organic ATM machine.

Relationships go south when a person finds himself or herself married to or involved with a "Mr. or Mrs. Know-It-All." The remark "often wrong but never in doubt" fits many of those who reign supreme at work but falter with their family.

Our reaction to difference is perhaps one of the biggest problems we face on planet earth. The ability to be open to divergent feedback is the key to opening the door to harmony. Be it international, national or on a personal level it is essential to find ways to open the closed mind. For some it requires an in-depth review of how our bio-computer got programmed and making a plan to reverse this devastating approach to the ones we love while they are still around us.

The closed mind may be factually right and may win the battle but will probably lose the war. If this is you, you can find a new approach to dealing with difference. I suggest, you organize, fight, and win with the love and understanding everyone is looking for deep down.

7. Respect yourself
(Never do what you know inside is not right)

If you think about it most all of us know right from wrong and what we really need and want. If this is true, and I believe it is true, why are so many people unhappy and doing such dumb things?

Many people get respect from job performance and the recognition that goes with it. This is true for many, perhaps for most of us. Some people build up their position by standing on the shoulders of others, pushing them down to elevate themselves, or so they thought. Unfortunately, these people are ubiquitous and are found in all professions and walks of life.

Insecurity is the breeding ground for this way of life. Self-respect translates operationally into true respect for self and that translates into actions that give respect to others.

8. Never lie to yourself
(About needs, desires or motivations)

Winston Churchill called it, "Terminological Inexactitude." Some call it "Disingenuous Behavior," while still others call it just plain

"Lying." Regardless of how colorful or exact the language is, we are all guilty of self-delusion at different times and to varying degrees.

In William Shakespeare's Hamlet, Polonius tells his son Laertes, "To thine own self be true, and it must follow, as the night the day, thou canst not then be false to any man."

It is hard to live a working life with "clinical logic" as a daily foundation of decision-making and have a personal life that may run on an entirely different premise. Human interactions cloud clarity much of the time. To the analytical mind denial and distance provide solace and sanctuary until logic can provide security once again in the work place.

Long hours relate to work demand but they may also relate to the haven provided by a world run on a different more stable and predictable logic. You would do well to take a close look at this idea.

A relationship is always getting better or worse. The direction of the arrow is the harbinger of happiness. Being able to see whether it's getting better or worse, in time, can save a marriage and provide a deeper meaning to life.

When you take the "Goodfield Interpersonal Values Evaluation Test" (GIVE) with your partner, you will be able to have an open discussion of the present direction of your relationship.

9. *Be who you are now*
(But be able and willing to change)

This is, in most cases, not a problem. What may be something to consider is how open you are to change within yourself. And how aware are you of the possible need to make that change.

I think one of the biggest sins of which a person can be guilty is to believe their "Terminological Inexactitude," or their own BS. When people around you constantly reinforce an image (not necessarily a reality) it is easy to believe the image over the human reality with all its frailties and frustrations.

In a daily life, where minor moves may have a major impact, finding a balance between home and office, can be hard. We all wear different "hats" daily. Husband, wife, parent, teacher, boss, secretaries, bank clerks etc., those "hats" can generate confusion at some times, yet they give clarity to others.

Our identity changes with time. It is usually subtle and in that sense requires periodic re-evaluation regarding goals and objectives. Motivations and meanings often evolve as well with subtlety. Our core usually remains stable, but the payoff we get from giving is important to balance against who we are and where the direction is taking us.

10. *Be your own best friend*
(Be kind, caring & loving to others)

This implies you know who you are first of all. "Are you your own best friend?" Some might look at this question and think that I'm crazy or have been in the Arizona sun too long.

Being your own best friend is directly related to the ability of other important people in your life to love and have deep contact with you. There is such a thing as "healthy narcissism". However, the "other" type of narcissism gets such a bad rap that the mere suggestion of the word makes some people pull their head back like a turtle under attack. A healthy appreciation of who you are is a good thing.

When the hub of any wheel is unstable or not "true" or in balance, the whole wheel's performance will suffer. So it is with people. Our stability relates to our own ability to manage all of the divergent pressures and expectations of the day and this is so true for all of us.

When consumed in a vortex of time and expectation, it is wise to stop sometime to take an accurate assessment of what you are doing and what it costs you.

This is where the GIVE test at the end of this book can help you.

Concluding thoughts

I have said and continue to say that the person you are and the skills you have honed and continue to improve daily are what set you apart from others. It is not just the lives you impact daily; many in other walks of life affect their world in a profound way with their actions as well. We are a kind of "tightrope walker", balancing professional skill with human contact. Failing to strike that balance, you will become disillusioned and indifferent to the critical tasks at hand. This is not the person you want to be. No, not at all.

When my son Eric turned eighteen, I gave him these words as a guide. They came to me in a dream, and I will share these words with you: "Be open, be honest, be loving, and be free. And let no person transgress with impunity."

KEYS TO A BETTER PERSONAL BALANCE WORKSHEET

Rank on a scale from 1 to 10 how well you practice (with 10 being maximum success on that point) and give a number to yourself as to how well you do on this point.

1. Clear boundary setting.
   (What I will and will not do)

2. Be here and now
   (With all the good and bad news that implies)

3. Trust your feelings
   (Accept them over others' reality)

4. Be able and willing to make contact
   (And in your own way)

5. Say what you feel
   (Value being clear over being liked)

6. Be open to difference
   (Hear things hard to hear while keeping your mouth shut and mind open)

7. Respect yourself
   (Never do what I know inside is not right)

8. Never lie to yourself
   (About needs, desires or motivations)

9. Be who you are now
   (But be able and willing to change)

10. Be your own best friend
    (Be kind, caring & loving to others)

24

Chapter 4

NECESSITIES FOR A LOVING, HEALTHY RELATIONSHIP

Trust, Honesty, Clarity, Goodwill, Give, Common Goals, Forgiveness, Truthfulness, Respect, Risk Taking, Spontaneity, Madness, Mystery and Fantasy as well as the "Big three Ls": Lust, Like and Love.

Let's look at them one at a time.

Trust

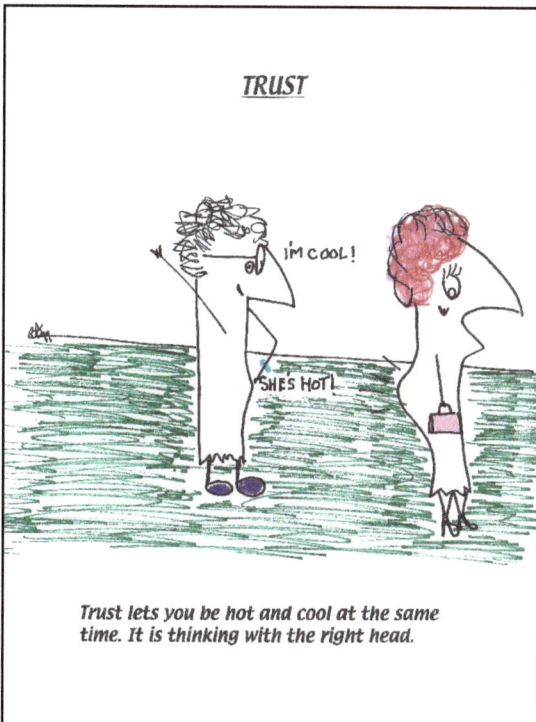

TRUST

Trust lets you be hot and cool at the same time. It is thinking with the right head.

By trust I mean first dealing with your core issues that taint, taunt and cause trouble on all levels of your life.

I have found that if you fail to deal with these, for whatever reason, the quality of life will always suffer. How can you ever let go if you are questioning the motivation, movements and meaning of another? How do you know if you have a problem in this area? Here is the answer to this question. All people do. ALL!

Life teaches us at one time or another that we are foolish to trust. The extent, intensity, and repetition of this message are the degree to which this will be a fundamental issue in your life. What should I do about the problem of "basic distrust"? Stop lying to yourself and stop projecting your issues onto other people. If you need to work on a problem, you know it already, so do it! This is especially true if you are in or just leaving a problematic relationship.

Honesty

Whoever said, "Honesty is the best policy" made no reference to the price tag. If honesty is a virtue, then we live in a world of vice and iniquity. A peek at any newspaper or a glance at any television or a scrupulous look at your day will prove my point. One of the first things I did in a budding relationship, was to pretend to be better or more virtuous than I was. That was not hard in my case. The consequence of this of course, was that my words were writing checks that my behavior could not cash.

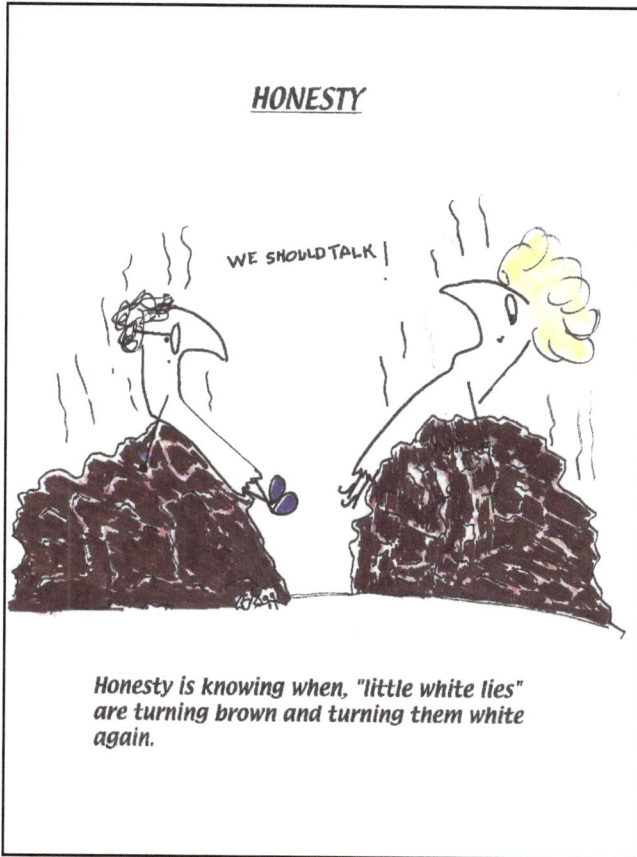

Honesty is knowing when, "little white lies" are turning brown and turning them white again.

I have learned that, as a principle, I would rather be clear than liked. Is this a natural strategy? No. This realization comes with age and, in my case, a nose that is not as straight as it was when I started out. Look, I am more interesting than I am nice. I guess it has always been that way. I am however, now, a very honest person. I walked a lot of really fine lady's down a primrose path.

So is honesty really the best policy? Here's my take on the subject. Sometimes you can get away with a lie, even a BIG one. For example the person with whom you are involved is having a relationship with somebody else. The person is not having a relationship with you. They are relating to you through the false reality they sold you. My dad used to say, "You can't build a castle on sand." One thing is sure the gritty truth will eventually come out. If you want to build that castle on a solid foundation, base it on truth and honesty.

For some people who do not choose this as a lifestyle, failure is a tick of the clock away and either denial or anxiety marks off the seconds.

I have found out that if I am really me in the beginning of any relationship, regardless of what kind it is, and the person dislikes me it is fine. He or she is doing me a favor by communicating this to me. I will not waste my time or theirs for that matter. Next! As one of my favorite philosophers Willie Nelson say, "He ain't wrong, he is just different." Tell it like it is. I have found it to be better that way.

Clarity

I have made my point and my position clear in the last section. One last thought or comment on the subject. "Why would someone choose to be vague or unclear?" My personal and clinical experience leads me to believe that, when this is a lifestyle, there are a few reasons behind this strategy. One reason is that the person is fundamentally insecure and is looking to another to define themselves or their actions. Another reason is that the person has a hidden agenda. When this is the case grab your valuables and run, don't walk to the nearest exit. Next NOW!

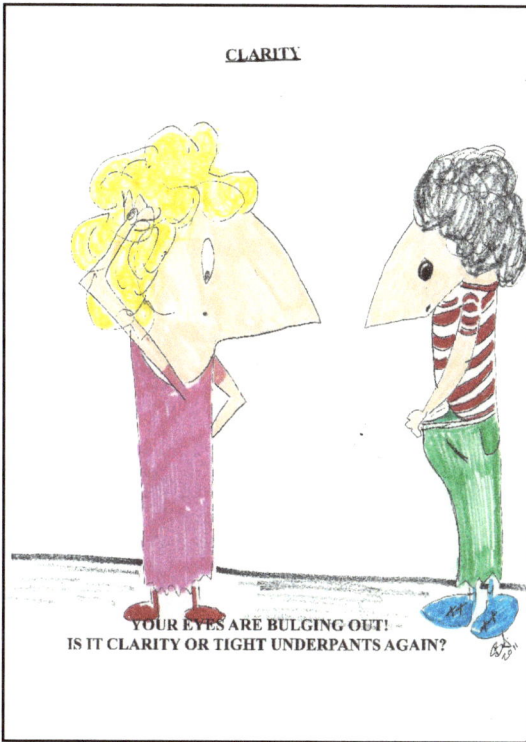

Goodwill

If a relationship is to survive life's seasons, goodwill is probably the most important currency to have. Goodwill accrues for those inevitable hard times that a couple must endure to get to those precious metal anniversaries. Goodwill is kindness and understanding. Sometimes in a relationship words and thoughts are sharp and painful, they cut the "U" out of "Us", leaving only a deep sense of longing and loneliness.

Goodwill is a special kind of long-term friendship.

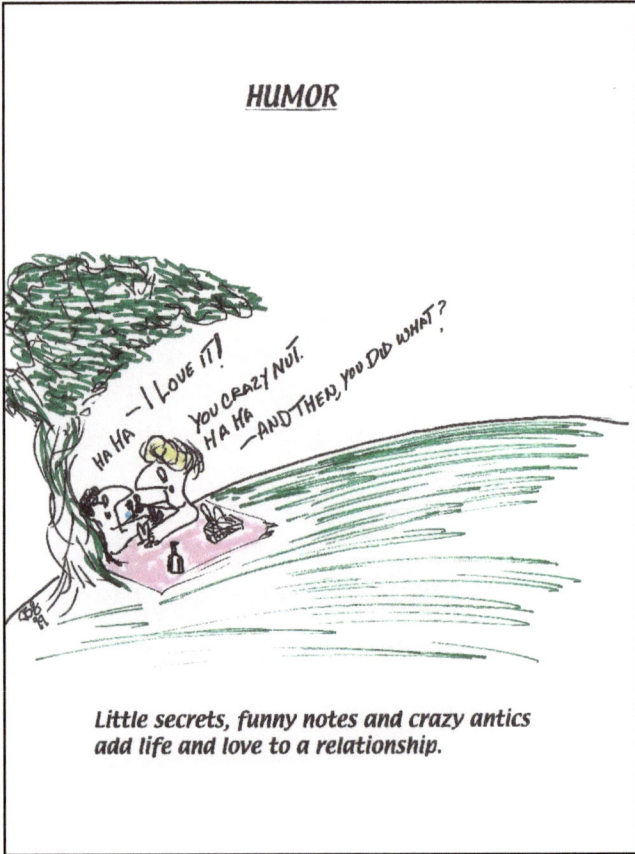

Little secrets, funny notes and crazy antics
add life and love to a relationship.

I know when it is there. I feel deep warmth and a kind of knowing smile when I look at the one I love being herself. It could be a look at a piece of fabric in a store, or a glance at me when I do that same old dumb thing. Whatever it is, goodwill is the long-term fuel essential in any relationship worthy of the name.

Common Goals

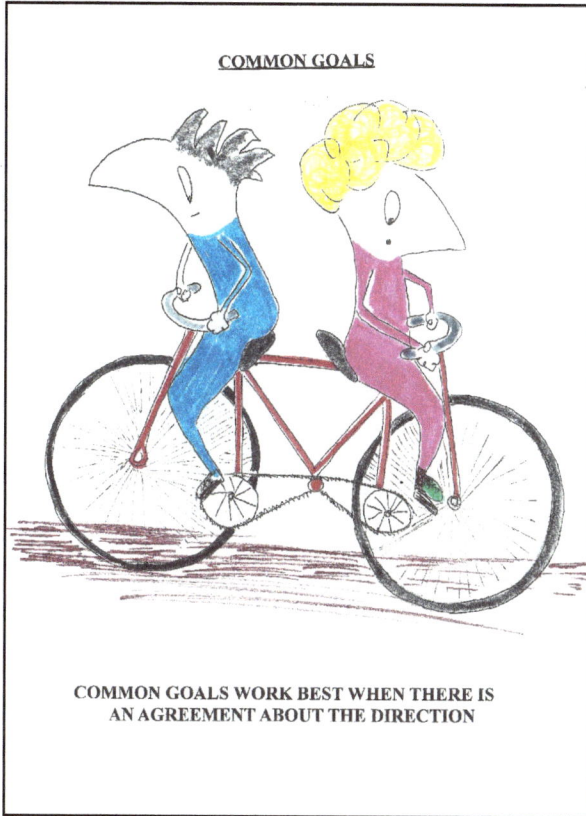

COMMON GOALS

COMMON GOALS WORK BEST WHEN THERE IS
AN AGREEMENT ABOUT THE DIRECTION

Goodwill is in direct proportion to the degree that there is a clear understanding or perception of what the common goals between the couple are. This is a knowledge that transgresses information. It is knowledge within and about a relationship that can evolve with time into a dynamic wisdom. It is a basic or fundamental awareness that we are one, a melting of fears, fantasies and hopes for fulfillment. This means difference not division, it means approaches that may not be the same, it means a viewpoint unique to each person that is not corrupted by bias or pressure to please or conform.

Common goals are key to my definition of love and friendship, which I have violated oh, so many times. It makes two people bigger together than they are apart. These are not just words now; they are words by which I live these days.

"What do I need to do to find them in another?" you ask. First, search for and then clarify your own real goals in life. Use whatever it takes to find them, a fortune cookie, a sage, the latest "get clear and happy" book or a good psychotherapist. Whatever you do, stop the bullshit and do it NOW! Be open, honest, clear, loving and free in what you do and say.

Forgiveness

When word and deed prove your humanness and folly in attempting to gratify your needs, there is only one thing left to do when honestly motivated to keep the relationship intact. Forgiveness. Sounds easy to say but perhaps it is the most difficult thing to do. This is because it requires a psychological juggling act that must become a habitual pattern of response. Every day and every night, forgiveness must win out over the need to punish either yourself or another. For me, the word has always been

NEXT. Break the agreement and I am out. End of story. This is the easy way to address pain and inflict punishment. This is my shortcoming, and I see it as such. As a psychologist, I have learned that, forgiveness is the key to living both in the here and now and in the there and then.

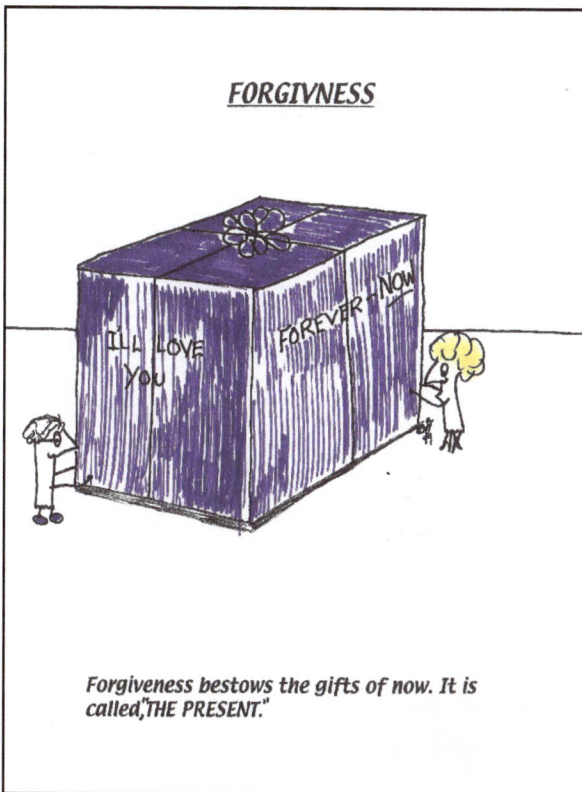

FORGIVNESS

Forgiveness bestows the gifts of now. It is called,"THE PRESENT."

Forgiveness is an acknowledgment of human need. And an acceptance that often our strategies at attempting to fulfill those needs are not always well thought out or well intended. What I know, as a professional and as a person, is that I cannot make someone's history go away. All I can offer is re-symbolization or forgiveness. I cannot make parents better than they were or spouses more faithful than they have been. All a person can do to make life move from retribution and wrangling past problems, promiscuity, and perceptions is to re-symbolize or, in other words, forgive. If a person cannot surmount this major challenge, then they owe it to themselves to walk out and give the other person a chance to find happiness somewhere else. If you stay without genuine forgiveness it is for the wrong reason and all should question their decision to stay in this self-created hell.

Truthfulness

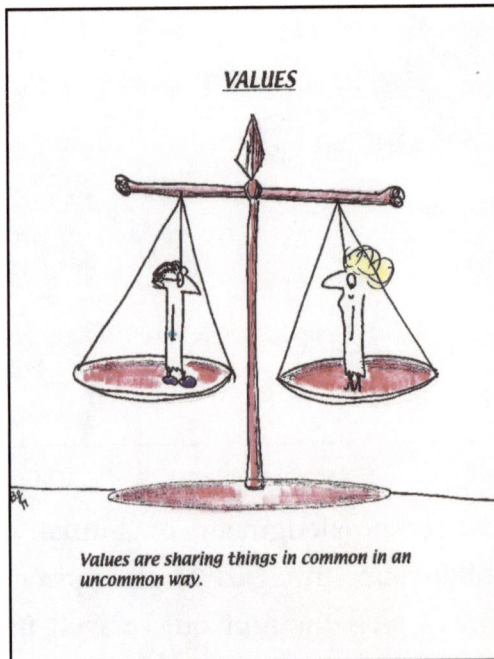

VALUES

Values are sharing things in common in an uncommon way.

A relationship will fail in proportion to the degree that there is dishonesty, deceit, or denial. As it was said earlier the "truth" or the lack thereof is the killer or antidote to the survival of a relationship.

All is perception, so why not share your own unique translation of the "facts" and your own awareness on what "reality" is.

If you are courageous enough, as I said earlier, to "tell it like it is", then the worst thing that can happen is that differences are seen in an amicable context of differing perceptions. This stops the killer strategy of holding feelings inside and waiting for the moment for payback. I once had a "lasting" long term relationship with a woman who was typing a paper for me. Instead of typing the word "psychology" she typed the word "spycology" instead. That said it all. She distrusted me, and the skills I was developing at that time.

This turned out to be a Freudian slip that heralded the basic distrust within our relationship. I got a clue about her distrust and pent up feeling as I left for the night shift at work one night. This quiet, passive lady buried a book 3/4 of an inch into a hollow door as I exited with a "warm goodnight."

I have learned that talking is not necessarily communication, and that communication is not necessarily understanding. Truthfulness is not the best policy in a relationship; it is the only policy if you want it to last. What starts as a little white lie can turn brown fast.

If you are afraid to tell the truth to your mate there are two possibilities.

One, you have strung together a necklace of lies that has chocked the truth out of you. In this case figure out how much you really care and decide if the price of a "new" relationship based upon truth is worth the pain and suffering of facing your past lies. This is big stuff, think about it before you act.

And second, can the relationship "handle" a close look at the reality upon which it was founded. If it is based upon compatible pathology, you will have a hard time realizing this as it is unconscious and, therefore, below your level of awareness. What usually happens in this case is that the relationship turns into a "relationshit." (My pal Wim mentioned this slip in his introduction to the book.) Therapy is the only real answer here, if you want to break free.

Respect

I have learned that respect, more than any other behavior, is perhaps on a deep level of consciousness the most important factor for woman. It is less so for men as when they have power especially in relation to woman they infer respect. This in itself can be the basis for a surprise later when she fails to do what he says. He sees it as a sudden cessation of power in relation to her, so more power is necessary. It is "*her*" failure to accept "*his*" power. She sees it as standing up to his disrespect. When this happens he is having one conversation or argument and she quite another. A high testosterone level, a silver tongue, one eye on the door, and a closed mind "protected" me from this insight for years. It's a macho man's ultimate shield.

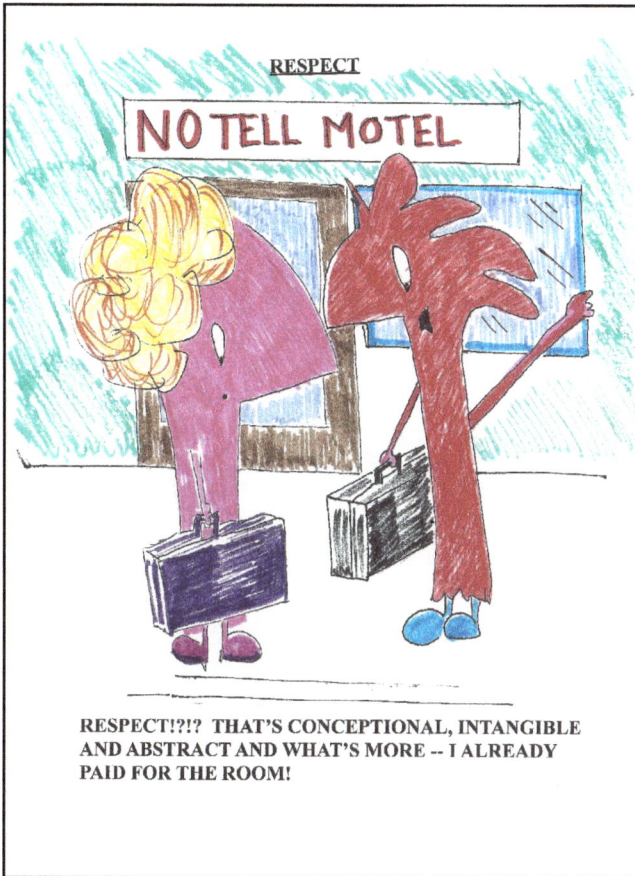

Respect is a word that is descriptive of daily behavior within a context. It ultimately boils down to actions. Here is the breeding ground for so many key factors in the success or failure within a relationship, such as trust, honesty, truthfulness, etc.

A woman puts a man into one of the two categories, he respects me or he doesn't.

Let us be clear, that when you are once categorized as one or the other, the die is cast in the relationship and movement from disrespect back to respect is difficult if not impossible. It's like trying to wash off an unwanted tattoo.

Risk Taking

Risk-taking in life is deciding how hard to press down on the accelerator and how many hands belong on the wheel. I have always believed that risk-taking is in direct proportion to growth. If you look at your list of personal hero's you are probably looking at the people who succeed at what you would like to do. When you consider what you admire in them it is more than likely, a large element of risk-taking on their part before they achieved their objective.

Risk-taking is a "'proof of life test" suggesting that you have found not only that there is life after birth but you have found ways to push the envelope. Risk-takers attract risk-takers and that is very important in a relationship.

If you are a person who is excited to discover what's around the next bend in life, you had better find a mate who has the same inquisitiveness and is comfortable with your seatbelts and driving skills.

Spontaneity

Spontaneity in a relationship is coupled with mystery, fantasy, and other activities that breathe life into the couple. It implies trust in each other and willingness to try new things, or the same things, but in a different way. You know you have chosen the right person for you, when you can both get into the car heading for one place, change your mind, head to another, change your mind again, and perhaps, even one final time and end up in a new place. While laughing and having fun about how the two of you fit so well together.

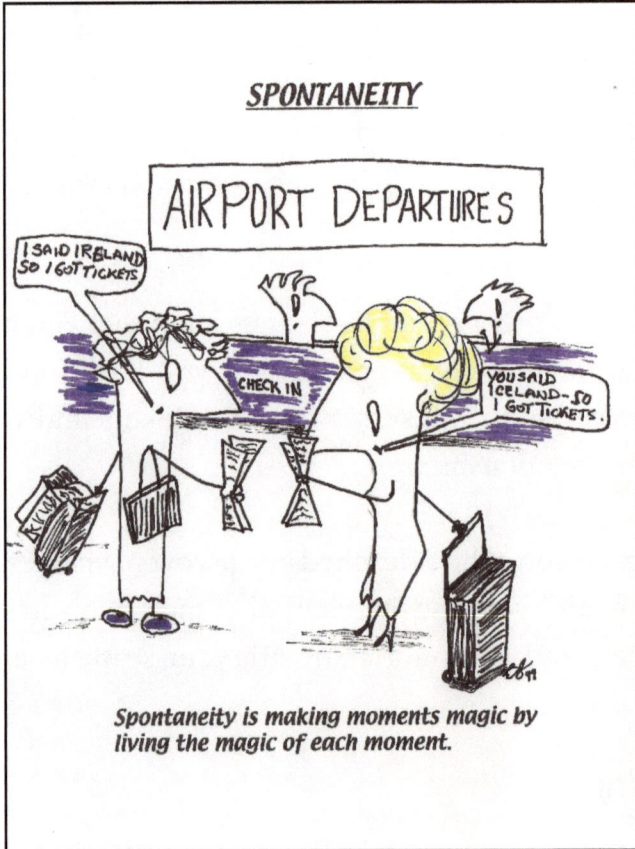

Spontaneity is making moments magic by living the magic of each moment.

Some couples need predictability. We all, on some level in our relationships, require predictability but when that becomes an obstacle to novelty and uniqueness of action this can be a sign of impending difficulty.

Madness

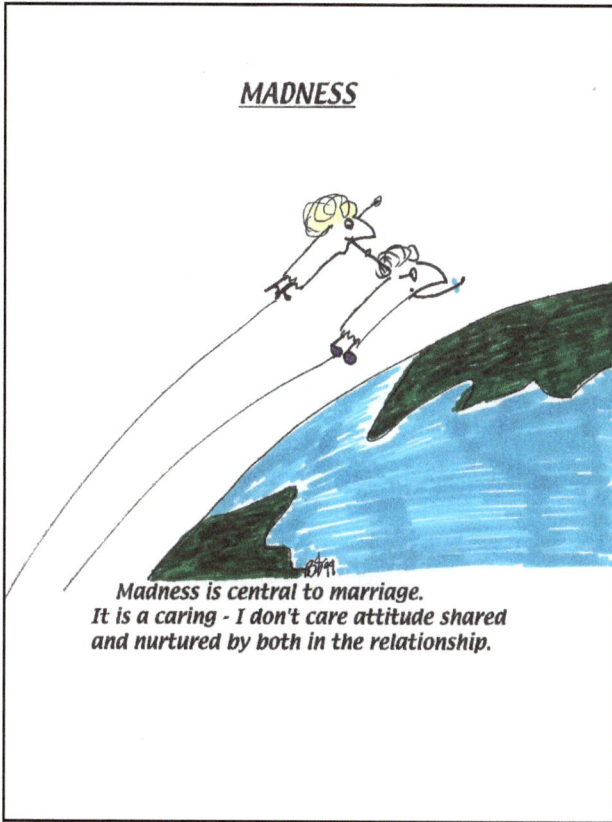

MADNESS

Madness is central to marriage.
It is a caring - I don't care attitude shared
and nurtured by both in the relationship.

In the 1964 movie *Zorba the Greek*, Alexis Zorba turns to the boss and says--,

"Dammit boss, I like you too much not to say it. You've got everything except one thing: madness! A man needs a little madness, or else...

Basil: Or else?

Alexis Zorba: ...he never dares cut the rope and be free."

Individual madness, in this sense, keeps you from going crazy and that was Zorba's message. In an interpersonal relationship madness is also essential. Madness is the Tabasco sauce on an otherwise tasteless taco. It operationally boils down to a kind of unpredictability between two people who have chosen to spend their life together.

In a relationship it's the individual feeling, the freedom to access his or her own impulsiveness, spontaneity, unpredictable outrageousness and share it with another.

Moreover, when it is between two people, it is a kind of created collective or cumulative self-concept. It develops together over time that says to the world, "You can count on us, to not be counted upon, to do what everybody else does. We have madness and passion within ourselves that we share freely with each other and the world. It is the "freedom glue" that holds a couple together.

Mystery

As discussed earlier mystery in a relationship relates to two important factors:

1. Living in the here and now
2. Maintaining an allure about yourself and your actions

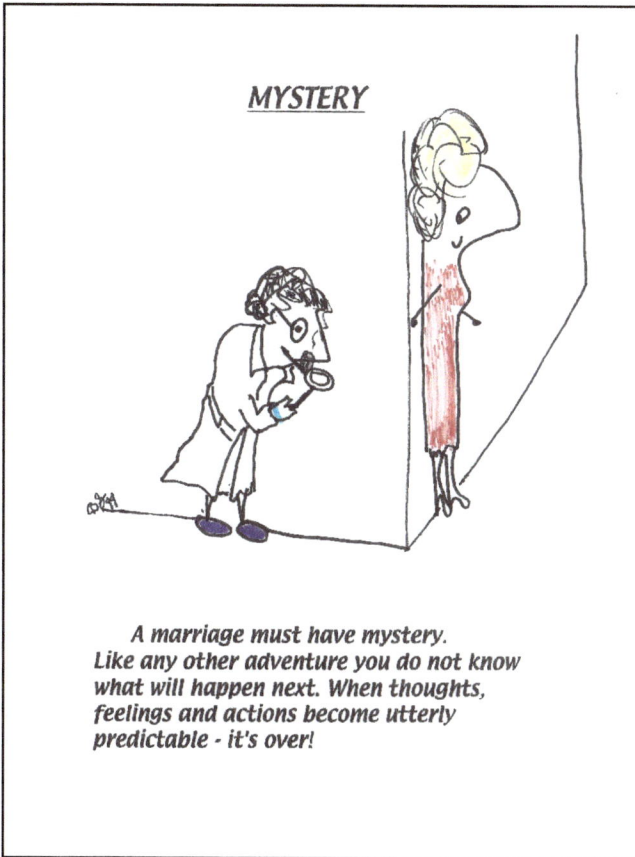

MYSTERY

A marriage must have mystery.
Like any other adventure you do not know
what will happen next. When thoughts,
feelings and actions become utterly
predictable - it's over!

Boredom is a killer of relationships. When a relationship becomes so predictable, that you can have an argument with somebody whether they are there or not, something is wrong.

One should never be able to safely say: "I know exactly what he or she will do or feel or how they will behave." The idea of finding a relationship like an old pair of shoes, to me, suggests something is run down and needs repair. It may fit swell but in the long run there is a place for warmth and there must be a place for fire. Any successful relationship must be able to provide both, lest it turn into a burned-out campfire.

Fantasy

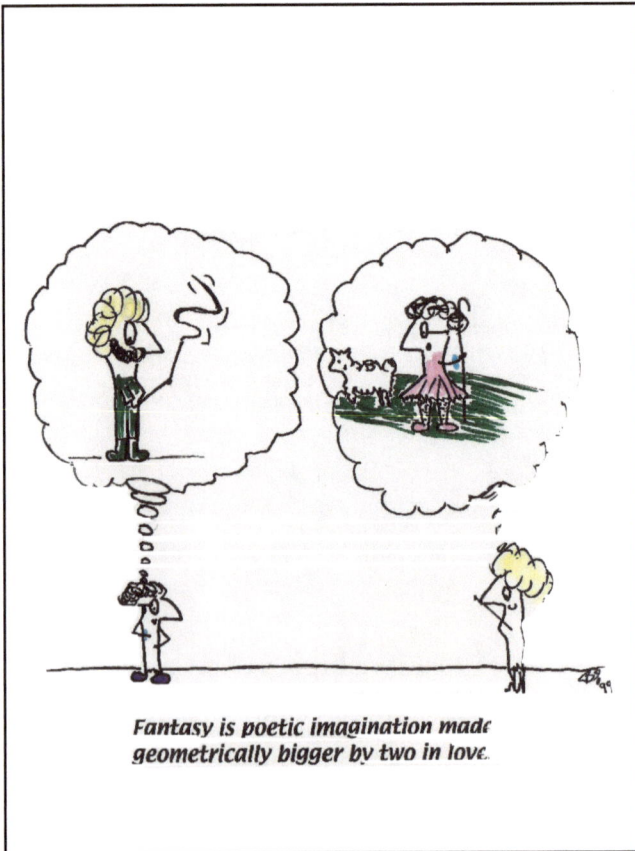

Fantasy is poetic imagination made geometrically bigger by two in love.

Fantasy in a relationship relates directly to fun. If a person is going to commit themselves to a long-term contact with anyone, the wide range of human emotion and needs, must be addressed on some level, in some mutually acceptable fashion.

Part of the maturing process in a relationship can be, and should be, the exploration of individual fantasies and wishes. They can range from adventures that one person always wanted to have and share. Be it a mountain to climb, a place to see for some time or an itch to scratch.

Of course, fantasies can and often do, relate to our sex life and de-sires. We reduce the possibility of infidelity in a relationship by sending a clear message about openness and desires. A fantasy is a picture, we paint in our mind, about a behavior yet unexplored or one we wish to revisit.

Most discussions about fantasies, when they relate to the behavior in the bedroom, often surface childhood anxieties and prohibitions about discussions we felt earlier in our life. It is important to share these ideas and learn your partner's boundaries and limitations, so that new roads and new adventures lay ahead of you both as you go forward together.

Now on to the "Big 3 Ls":

Lust

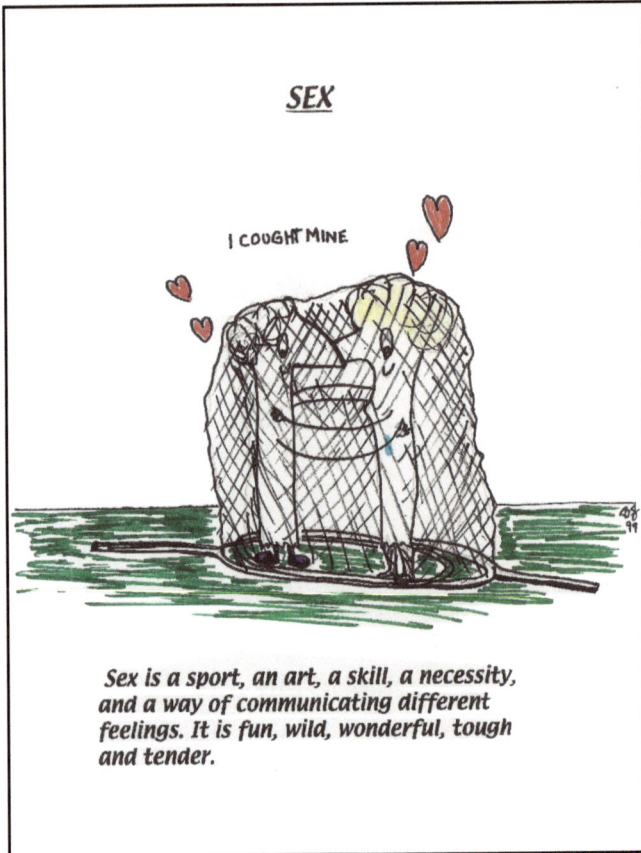

SEX

I COUGHT MINE

Sex is a sport, an art, a skill, a necessity, and a way of communicating different feelings. It is fun, wild, wonderful, tough and tender.

Lust is that longing in the loins that bypasses rational reason. It is the point of passion rarely felt by most and often silently hoped for by the many. When Thoreau said, "The mass of men (most people) lead lives of quiet desperation", he could have been peeking directly into the secret fantasy lives of humanity. We fear to act and so we fantasize with pornography, soft and hard, in the glamorous lights of sexy advertising or the dim and darkness of "dirty" thoughts or dastardly deeds.

Sex is great whether it is with silk and whispers or groans and sweat. For many it is a kind of proof of both me and you. It proves "me" as desirable, capable, and able to please, pleasure and procreate. It proves "you" as able, willing and open to me. Lust as a part of a relationship is so often down-played by those who see themselves as educated, refined, or above that basic behavior of the bedroom. Those who present themselves this way are lying first to themselves and second to anyone foolish enough to hear and believe their nonsense.

So what should a person do with their lustful feeling towards somebody outside the relationship? There are two basic possibilities; to act or not to act. To act is to attempt to translate fiction to fact. There will always be consequences when fiction becomes fact. It will be major or minor depending on your present circumstances. I have often acted on these impulses like a blind man running on a tight rope without a net. You do not always need a net in life but good judgment is important.

The problem occurs when the fall happens, and in most cases it does, more than one person is seriously injured. I have learned that living in the here and now does not necessarily means acting on all possibilities. It means noting possibilities and using good judgment regarding them.

What should I do when I am smitten? Excuse yourself and go to the restroom. Pull out your wallet and look at the pictures of those with whom you have made a contract about your emotions. Decide how much this behavior will cost. Decide if you are willing to pay the price if things go wrong. If you get a green light think about making a phone call and telling your loved one, whose picture is lodged in your wallet or purse, of your intentions. If you cannot do this go home and have a serious conversation about your intended actions and your frustrated lustful feelings.

Tough assignment but better than the predictable consequences.

Like

FRIENDSHIP

Friendship is liking the cut of each other's jib and fantail too. It's two people bigger together than they are when they are apart.

Much has already been said about the importance of "like" in a relationship in previous sections-- but here are a few more thoughts. When a relationship is based upon "like," there is an implied knowledge of the other person. When you do not really like the other person and you continue to continue your involvement you can be sure of one thing, the unconscious is steering your doomed ship.

If a relationship is going to last, "like" had better be a key to your commitment. Like includes an awareness of what the person is really all about in thought and action. Would you want to spend time getting to know his or her innermost thoughts or feelings? If the answer is anything other than a resounding unequivocal "yes" excuse yourself and this time smile, give your excuses, and walk to the door.

Love

When people think of "love," in most cases they think of being loved by a person they like, their parents or children. In other words, they think of receiving love. This kind of thinking needs to be changed. If everyone wants to receive love, and no one is left to give, this will lead to a worldwide shortage of love.

It is important first to supply love. If everyone supplies love, then the world will be filled with love. You need to stop thinking only of what you can take or get.

A FEW THINGS LOVE IS:

1. LOVE IS SINGING SONGS TOGETHER
2. LOVE IS PLAYING DUMB GAMES
3. LOVE IS GIVING GIFTS FOR NO REASON
4. LOVE IS NOT GIVING INTO YOUR ANGER
5. LOVE IS KNOWING WHEN TO REMEMBER AND TO FORGET
6. LOVE IS BEING HIS/HER PERSONAL FOOL
7. LOVE IS BEING THERE FOR EACH OTHER
8. LOVE IS BOTH OF YOU LIVING IN THE HERE AND NOW
9. LOVE IS LAUGHING AT THE SAME OLD DUMB JOKES
10. LOVE IS SURPRISING EACH OTHER
11. LOVE IS LONG ROMANTIC DINNERS
12. LOVE IS LET HER/HIM HAVE THE "FLIPPER" TO THE T.V.
13. LOVE IS HAVING "LITTLE SECRETS" TOGETHER
14. LOVE IS EATING A BAD MEAL AND KEEPING YOUR MOUTH SHUT
15. LOVE IS NOT BEING TOO PREDICTABLE
16. LOVE IS NOT USING ALL THE HOT WATER
17. LOVE IS BEING ABLE TO SHUT UP AND LISTEN
18. LOVE IS A "LITTLE WHITE LIE" SOMETIMES (HAIR, CLOTHS)
19. LOVE IS ALWAYS TELLING THE TRUTH (EXCEPT NO. 18)
20. LOVE IS BEING EACH OTHERS HERO

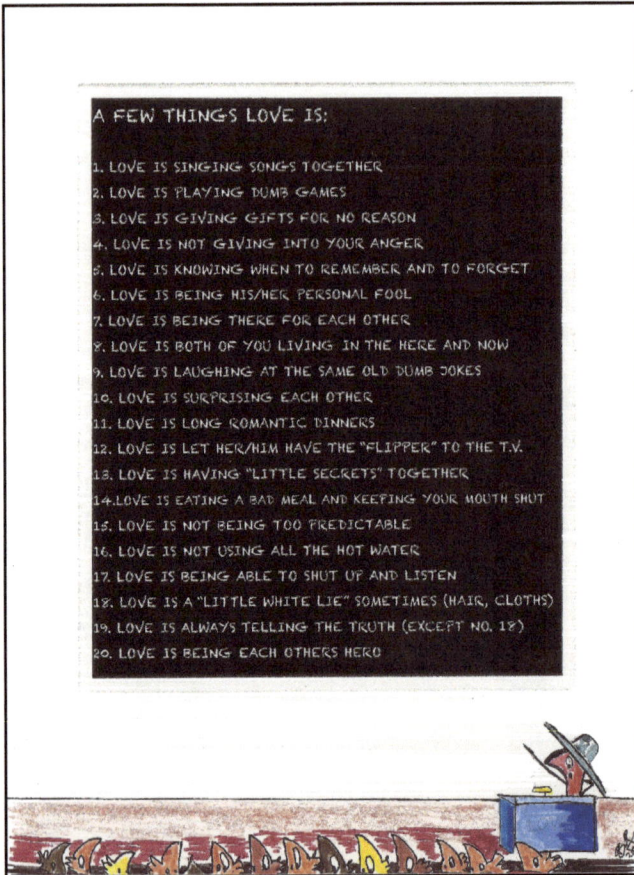

Being able to receive is just as important in a relationship as it is to give.

If you are a great giver, but have a hard time receiving, you may be able to love. On the other hand it makes it hard for the other person to feel that their love and caring is being received.

One of the only true statements that can be said in a marriage or any long-term commitment is that "I will love you forever – now". If this is not true, there wouldn't be a sky-rocketing divorce rate. Russian roulette would be a statistically better bet than marriage, where the chances are one in six of bang verses click. While marriage is now a flip of the coin with a 50% chance of failure.

But, on the other hand, there is a 50% chance of success also. Those chances are significantly improved when the promise at the altar is a dynamic and genuine commitment to act, rather than a static sentence. There is hope for you and a successful relationship.

If you are in a terminal relationship, for your sake as well as any children that might be involved, stop lying to yourself. Stop committing suicide, a centimeter at a time, and take action. Be sure that your spouse has not damaged your self-confidence, this happens in the majority of the time.

Know that you are a worthwhile person regardless of all the slings and arrows shot in the last act of a failing relationship.

And never forget the Golden Rule: "Treat others the way you would like to be treated yourself."

Love is based upon openness, vulnerability, contact and kindness. It is in you.

The "L" with the relationship

Here are 3 to consider:

Like: is based upon similar views
is based upon similar values
is based upon similar venues
is based upon similar ventures

Lust: is based upon compatible chemistry
is based upon pulsing passion
is based upon teasing tensions
is based upon fabulous fantasies
is based upon tantalizing time tidbits

Love: is based upon tender touch
is based upon warm wishes
is based upon romantic realities
is based upon transforming time
is based upon building balance

What happens when one "L" dominates a relationship?

Like, lust and love are based on the following keystones.
Here are 3 things to consider:

LIKE
When a relationship is ruled by Like thinking is key
When a relationship is ruled by Like perceptions prevail
When a relationship is ruled by Like rationality rules
When a relationship is ruled by Like will and wit win
When a relationship is ruled by Like legitimacy lingers

LUST
When a relationship is ruled by Lust caution can't count
When a relationship is ruled by Lust moments are magnified
When a relationship is ruled by Lust impulse invalidates insight
When a relationship is ruled by Lust flesh is always first
When a relationship is ruled by Lust sin sings sensuous songs

LOVE
When a relationship is ruled by Love respect rules
When a relationship is ruled by Love balance is bliss
When a relationship is ruled by Love tenderness is tops
When a relationship is ruled by Love touching is terrific
When a relationship is ruled by Love the future is forever, NOW

Giving

One of the basic principles in psychology is that all behavior is motivated by something. People do things for a reason. There is, on the other hand, the notion of magnanimity. Or in other words, giving and sacrifice for another without any expectation whatsoever. When we see this consistently as a lifestyle of a regular person we think of people like Mother Theresa, Mahatma Gandhi, Martin Luther King, etc.

The issue is that, as I said, all behavior is motivated by an agenda. There's absolutely nothing wrong with this. We can do great things for others.

If you stay with the notion that all behavior is motivated, realize that sometimes "good people do bad things" and "bad people do good things." The reason, the bad and good things are put in quotation marks is, that it is a product of our perception in the context in which an action takes place.

There can be no doubt that some actions can only be seen as self-sacrificing and beyond the norm for all people. That is why, each country has special military decorations reserved especially for people who go beyond the call of duty. Each Medal of Honor, each Victoria Cross as a tribute to those brave and selfless people who sacrifice on behalf of others.

But if we were to issue medals to non-military men and women for their self-sacrifice, many ordinary moms, dads, and grandparents would have a wall full of them.

Parent's sacrifice for their children every day and, it is safe to say, that loved ones do this for their family and friends regularly. To some, the actions are extraordinary, to others, normal. But what we appreciate when we recognize this behavior, regardless of the context, is the idea that one gives beyond that which is expected.

Some would say this is part of the definition of love. Others would say it's simply a reflection of a certain type of character. I believe, that all people, ultimately and in the right context, have a great capacity to give, to share, and to open themselves in a way that shows not just vulnerability but a willingness to go beyond the bounds of that which is required and normally expected.

This process is called giving. When we see it as an unique way of reacting to one person or one group, as I said, we may see it as love, as a commitment, or simply as something special.

When we see it as a normal pattern, held by an individual, we think it is a lifestyle. Unfortunately, people like this, who we all know, are often taken advantage of, or treated in an inconsiderate way. Simply put, their boundaries are not respected and are regularly transgressed. And much of the time these individuals do not speak up nor stand up for themselves and their rights.

Here we usually find a caring friend or relative, who finds themselves in the protective role, trying to defend the boundaries of someone else, but refuses to defend themselves.

I'd like you consider the amount of time, energy and research that you put into buying your last computer. You compare performance with price, features with ease-of-use and generally, cost versus benefit.

Perhaps the same level of discrimination might improve the chances of finding the love and happiness we all desire. It is in that spirit that I present some questions that you might want to address before you make an investment even greater than the one you made with the computer that you currently have.

Here are some questions to ask yourself before you try to save your relationship:

> Do you love this person?
> Do you like this person?
> Do you respect this person?
> Do you trust this person?
> Do you like having sex with this person?

Here are some pre-questions to ask yourself about what you think your partner feels about you:

> Do they love you?
> Do they like you?
> Do they respect you?
> Do they trust you?
> Do they like having sex with you?

1) Do you love this person?

If you cannot answer this question honestly, it may say more about the mess you both have made than what may lie buried under all of the uproar you created.

The pre-questions are critical to be clear about after all it's your life. My experience tells me this when a relationship is in serious trouble much of the time neither partner has the basis for a marriage or a divorce.

Relationships rarely get in trouble over one thing; it is usually a collective daily effort on both people part. If this is the case, then just how do you go about decoding the mass?

Perhaps a useful approach would be to go back to the beginning of the relationship. This is the time when fantasy and fiction fill the air with happiness and hope. It is the glow that songwriters write about when everything seemed possible.

Later of course, saloon singers like Frank Sinatra sang songs about dashed hopes despair and late hours as he stared into a whiskey glass lamenting what was versus what would have been.

Get the context clear just where were you in your life at the time that that special person walking in and changed everything? As you know by now it is my fundamental belief that the goal of life is balance.

How much balance did you feel prior to the time you began the relationship? I believe this is a fundamental question because it addresses our need as people to have balance in life.

A relationship does not give balance it affects balance. If you had stability before the relationship began than you have avoided one of the fundamental problems I have seen with couples.

It bears repeating again; in a relationship to halves do not make a whole. When a person enters a relationship to escape his life situation, it is only a matter of time before there is a rendezvous with the past. And, when this occurs, it is usually an even bigger, pain-filled disappointment.

Make a list of five good things that have come from this relationship. Although you may be tempted to list children, friends and pets don't. Avoid this simple temptation. List what you feel are the positive emotional developments that have resulted from of being with your partner.

When you have completed this list it is time to honestly itemize five negative things that have developed during your time together. Here it is important to carefully examine your role in the emotional shipwreck that has become your relationship.

It is important to remember that all relationships, and people, are changing everyday - they are either getting better or they are getting worse. The sooner you can catch the direction of the arrow, the greater the chance you have of bringing about change when necessary.

2) Do you like this person?

It may seem difficult to believe, but it is quite possible to have evolution without revolutions. As the fiery passions of a new relationship evolve into a kindling flame and sometimes a lasting glowing ember, our feelings and needs and desires change.

It is my experience that perhaps the most important thing in a relationship is that you like the person you love. In other words, the most important thing is friendship. People fall out of love and like regularly. Much of the time this has to do with a lack of respect and appreciation for the strategies, held by each other, regarding life's differences and challenges.

Differences in perception and approach with time can erode like and love to the point where the person simply says this relationship costs me too much in terms of the benefit derived.

Here is where our fantasy of our chosen partner turns into a blueprint that foretells the life that we might construct together. It is at this crossroad where decisions are made. Sometimes we are not even aware it is taking place on a conscious level. It may simply feel like a continued disappointment and dissatisfaction.

Unfortunately, the truth and wisdom of our choices is not presented immediately; it is deduced logically with time. If incompatible values and strategies have led you to the conclusion that you do not like your partner it may be time to move on.

It is important to remember, that when the relationship is in crisis, good luck and good judgment are often on holiday somewhere else. If you find yourself in "deep like" with your partner you have the basis for rebuilding a damaged love relationship. Let us be clear however, "like" is never a satisfactory substitute for love in the long run. But it is critically important.

3) Do you respect this person?

If you do not respect your partner it may say as much about you as it does about your partner. The cornerstone of any good relationship is when each person has self-respect. If you don't respect yourself you really cannot respect another.

Respect has a lot to do with an appreciation of the decision-making process of another person. This is particularly important if that person plays a significant role in your daily life. We have an expression here in Arizona that says "You can't fix dumb." If you regularly feel that the decisions and directions taken by your partner are unintelligent, inappropriate or less than insightful, you may be sure the concept of respect is in serious jeopardy.

One thing that you might do is to ask your partner to name a few people that they admire. Look at their appreciation list and think about one of your own. This can produce some valuable information regarding compatibility. Don't forget, context determines meaning and perception determines reality. Asking this question at a racetrack can produce a different answer than asking this question when leaving church or synagogue. Nevertheless, we can put an arrow on the road to traveling.

Sometimes when a person is in a bad relationship, their self-respect is damaged and may have been, increasingly damaged to the point where they feel they may have lost their own identity.

When this is the case it would be a wise decision, before taking any major decision of your own, to repair the damage done to your self-concept and subsequently your self-respect.

There are many people, including close friends who can be helpful in this area. If however, you feel you are getting positive platitudes and not practical advice it might be time to seek professional help. For God sakes, pay attention to what I just wrote and do something about it if you need to.

If you do not respect your partner, it might be a wise idea to again make a list for yourself of those things which you do not respect in the interaction between you and your partner.

When people are in pain, judgment is impaired as our immediate desire is to reduce the pain and then address the problem. That's natural and normal. Things will not improve unless and until you address this critical component in a relationship. Unfortunately, once the pain has subsided, we sometimes fail to address the causality and, of course, when this happens, it's only a matter of time before the situation is repeated. If you've got a stone in your boot, the sooner you take it out the more pleasant will be your journey. Simple but like many simple thoughts - it's true.

I have seen so many people over the years "beaten down" both figuratively and literally. It is a painful thing to witness and surely even more painful to experience oneself. There comes a time in life when you have to weigh the costs versus the benefits. Judging the respect in a relationship is a good way to measure the health of any relationship.

4) Do you trust this person?

Trust is to a relationship like fuel is to a car. Without it you are not going to go very far. Once again, if you do not trust yourself you will have difficulty trusting another.

If, however, you have confidence in yourself and find that the confidence you invested in your partner was ill-spent, the result will be self-doubt. It's pretty hard to find your direction when you don't trust the compass you have been using. Here again adjustments and recalibration may be appropriate.

Distrust in a relationship is a silent cancer within the couple. Like any catastrophic disease it must be addressed quickly and thoroughly. You must explore the underlying causality - the sooner the better! Distrust will pull a relationship apart and erode any good will still remaining in the relationship.

In most cases a relationship does not begin with distrust. It is therefore wise to figure out when trust turned to distrust. Often times this relates to extramarital affairs or some form of perceived infidelity.

When this is the case go into therapy until both of you agree the issues have been successfully addressed. Most people would agree that, as they get on with their life, the most important thing in their life is perhaps the relationships they have developed both personally and professionally.

I think it's safe to say, married, living together or simply an intense personal involvement is at the top of that list.

5) Do you like sex with that person?

Sex represents many things in a relationship, but it is one of the most important communication barometers about you and the person with whom you are involved. As I said before - sex is many different things. It is a sport, skill, necessity, a way of showing different feelings. It is fun, wild, wonderful, tough, tender, dirty, and spiritual.

Needless to say, this list could go on and on. The context of a sexual encounter will profoundly influence the definition that you give to that time together.

First sexual experiences are notoriously filled with anxiety and misgivings. Moreover, with all the pressures and expectations that go with the first time event it is no wonder that in most cases it is disappointing. Most folks are just happy to get it over with so they can begin to address the issue of sexuality with a more realistic expectation.

There comes a time in a sexual relationship when you stop looking at your own performance and trepidations, and begin to honestly address your feelings about your partner. This is your moment of truth. It is a time when hopes and happenstance are confronted by the reality you have with the person that you have chosen to share your bed.

It is unrealistic to believe that you can have a good sexual relationship with someone with whom you have poor communication. Because the sexual act begins with a certain level of vulnerability. If you do not express your feelings when you have your clothes on, it will be even more harder when you have your clothes off.

If you do not feel comfortable or compatible with your sexual partner, it may reflect the fact that the two of you have not discussed honestly and openly your needs, preferences, and desires.

Consider reviewing the section on love, lust, and like with these principles in mind. It is difficult to be tender when there is unresolved anger in the relationship. It is difficult to feel close when distrust characterizes your interactions. It is difficult to feel excitement when anxiety reflects the fear in your relationship. It is difficult to feel sexually free in your relationship when negative judgments are part of your daily contact.

Reviewing these principles, notice how many of them relate to communication and goodwill. If you had that before, and you do not have it now, something has gone wrong in your communication with your partner. Only you can decide whether or not you want to make the investment to improve the contact. Whether you know it or not, you are the boss and whatever you do show your partner what you really feel.

As Lancelot said in Shakespeare's Merchant of Venice, "Truth will out."

A more contemporary and less eloquent way of communicating the same message is, "Tell it like it is!" One way or another, what you really feel shows - so you might as well talk about it because it is the only way to make something better.

Now take the same questions and answer them as you feel your partner would when asked about their feelings about you.

When you've done this share this with your partner.

How does this relate to the GIVE test, which I hope, you will take with somebody important in your life?

It will surface the agenda on both conscious and an unconscious level. It will also reveal the level of commitment that each individual has to that special relationship. Perhaps the most important benefit that will result from exploring the relationship using the GIVE test, is the fact that communication will take place around the areas where communication is most needed, and perhaps been most absent. If one honestly and openly enters into this endeavor, with an open mind and a willingness to be clear about their feelings and ideas, I have no doubt that you will come away feeling you got more than you gave.

All people have the choice to decide how much of themselves they are going to show to another. The GIVE test will shine the light on this issue as well. I wish you good luck and simply say that honesty and openness are in direct proportion to the degree you are willing to give it yourself. Give, Give, Give!

There is one more thing I want to say: "Trust your process, it will work. I'm still in process and I am trusting mine."

68

Chapter 5

Goodfield Interpersonal Values Evaluation

(GIVE)

It is not essential that you have read *"Relationships: A Survival Guide"* to take the Give test. It would however, better prepare you for an in-depth exploration of the issues, concerns, and obstacles that you may see in your current relationship with your partner.

As I said, it is not essential, but might be useful. Regardless of this factor, as Winston Churchill said, "Come then, let us go forward together with our united strength."

Some years ago I developed a test to surface a person's place within his or her interpersonal relationship. There are lots of different types of relationships. We establish relationships with many different kinds of people, family members, neighbors, co-workers, friends, spouses, significant others, etc. As these contacts deepen and become a relationship, conflict can and does occur at different times.

One good way to clarify differences and to avoid conflicts, is to take this informative test with your partner. What is abundantly clear to me is that the goal of life is balance. It is possible to maintain balance at home when there is imbalance at work or vice versa, but not for long. It is only a question of time when personal imbalances, whether they are intra-psychic or interpersonal, will impact the performance on both fronts.

It is difficult and sometimes downright impossible to maintain balance, when, in your perception, the "rules" of the relationship seem to change like sand shifting under your feet. So what do you need? The answer is simple. Information!

Unfortunately, most significant relationships in our life do not begin with a detailed analysis of the underlying assumptions, that both people have. This is an important foundation for involvement or a serious commitment. Given this unfortunate reality, now might be a good time to raise the psychological hood on the vehicle that the two of you have created.

Why the GIVE test?

This should be the first thing you do before slipping a ring on another's finger.

This should be the "last chance" action before taking any provocative action like divorce, separation or throwing your hands up and just walking away.

This is the "Hail Mary" pass you should try when hope has left and is replaced by despair and foreboding.

Who should take the GIVE test?

- People considering marriage
- People considering divorce
- People who feel their relationship is growing "stale."
- People who feel their relationship is becoming boring
- People who feel their relationship needs to change somehow and need new direction, but that direction is not clear
- People who want to discover where the "fire" and passion went and notice, that what they have, is in danger of becoming a burnt out campfire

What should my partner and I do to prepare to take the GIVE test?

First agree that you are both willing to invest the time and energy to take a serious look at your relationship. There is no point doing this if you will not approach it with honesty and a genuine desire to learn more about the person with whom you are involved.

Even if you are considering ending the relationship, you do yourself a great service, by learning exactly why you are considering this course of action. Moreover, you may find that some of the differences and obstacles that seem so insurmountable now are in fact rooted in misperception, misunderstanding, and misinformation. Being clear about the above we are now ready to proceed to the discovery process.

How do we begin the GIVE test?

Turn off all cell phones, computers, or any other gadget which could inter-fere with this important effort! Make clear to any individuals in your im-mediate proximity that you must not be disturbed! No exceptions!

Find a quiet place where you will not be disturbed and follow the instructions exactly. Each person is to take approximately five minutes (give or take a minute or two but no more) per section. <u>Do not discuss</u> your responses until you and your partner have both completed the entire test. Upon completion, exchange papers with your partner and systematically discuss each section in an amen-able way before proceeding to the next one.

Remember, risk-taking is in direct proportion to growth. Also be clear that you are showing concern about the relationship by parti-cipating in this exercise. That fact itself deserves respect. Moreover, you are communicating how important the relationship is to both of you. That may be all it takes to make a good relationship even better, or to put a troubled one back on track.

While participating in this exercise, keep in mind that the goal --- as it is in life --- is the process and not the end result. This is not to say that, after taking the test, it may not affect the quality and end result of your contact. In most cases it does.

What is sure, your future actions are based on a clearer understanding of the motivational factors behind your partner's actions. Many couples in conflict don't have the basis for a good marriage or divorce simply because they do not know the facts of the situation.

Let's begin. Get two pens and paper.

74

Goodfield Interpersonal Values Evaluation

(*GIVE*)

SECTION ONE
Write down 10 sentences that reflect the goals you have now and hope to achieve within the next five years.

SECTION TWO
Write 10 sentences that begin with the words, "I am... "

SECTION THREE

10 sentences that begin with the words, "I need... "

SECTION FOUR

Write 10 sentences that begin with the words, "I am concerned (or anxious) about......"

SECTION FIVE
Repeat sections one through four, responding this time as you feel your partner would respond.

SECTION SIX
Rank by priority all ten sentences in section 1-5. The most import-ant will be1, second most important is 2, and so on.

SECTION SEVEN

Look at each section and write one sentence for each section that captures the feeling tone of that section.

SECTION EIGHT

Look at the four sentences that you wrote about yourself, and the four sentences you wrote about your partner in section seven, synthesize (combine) the four sentences about yourself and the four sentences about your partner into two sentences.

SECTION NINE

Exchange papers and discuss one section at a time, start with section one and work forward. Give each section the time necessary that *both* of you feel it requires.

SECTION TEN

Now that you both have new insight into your relationship, say or do something to reflect this new understanding in a positive way. If there are new decisions to be made and or different strategies to be taken between the two of you, write them down and make a copy for your partner.

References

Churchill. Winston
    Phrase *"Terminological Inexactitude"* first used during 1906 election

Churchill. Winston
    "Come then, let us go forward together with our united strength." May 13, 1940

Einstein. Albert
    "Men marry women with the hope that they will never change. Women marry men with the hope they will change. Invariably they are both disappointed."

Goodfield. Barry A.
    "Be open, be honest, be loving, and be free. And let no person transgress with impunity".

Goodfield. Barry A.
    <u>Insight & Action: The role of the unconscious in crisis from the personal to international levels</u>.
    University of Westminster, London, 1999 ISBN 1859191061

Hayakawa, S.I.
    <u>Language in Thought and Action</u> (fifth ed., 1990, Harcourt Brace & Company, NY,   NY) ISBN 0156482401.

Nelson. Willie
    Song "Mamas Don't Let Your Babies Grow Up To Be Cowboys" *"He ain't wrong, he is just different"*

Rogers. Kenny
  Song the Gambler, *"It's knowing when to hold them and knowing when to fold them."*

Shakespeare. William
  Hamlet written between 1599 and 1601

Thoreau. Henry David
  (born David Henry Thoreau; July 12, 1917 - May 6, 1862)
  Walden 1854

Tsongas. Paul
  (February 14, 1941- January 18, 1997)

Whitman. Walt
  Leaves Of Grass, 1855

Wikipedia, the free encyclopedia
  Temple of Apollo (Delphi)
  http://en.wikipedia.org/wiki/Delphi#Temple_of_Apollo

Zorba. Alexis
  Zorba the Greek, 1964 Movie
  Alexis Zorbas (original title)

About the Author

Prof. Barry Austin Goodfield, Ph.D., DABFM*

Prof. Goodfield is Founding Director of The Goodfield Institute LLC in Arizona, and The Netherlands. He holds a Ph.D. in Psychology and Human Behavior. In 1996 he became President & CEO of The Goodfield Foundation: for the Study of Conflict Communication and Peace Building. In 2010 he became President and CEO of The Goodfield Media Group International LLC.

Dr. Goodfield is also a Senior Professor at Henley-Putnam University instructing doctoral level students from the intelligence, and counter-terrorism community. He is a Family, Marriage and Child Therapist, international lecturer, author and noted radio and television personality. While a visiting Professor at the Diplomatic Academy of London he wrote the books _Insight and Action: The role of the unconscious in crisis from the personal to international levels_. His second book, _So you want to be my President? The ultimate voters'_ _guide_, has been published in 2011.

Prof. Goodfield holds two US patents on his psychotherapeutic process relating to analyzing the Non-Verbal Leak (NVL). He shared the Goodfield Method with psychiatrists, psychologists, social workers, senior corporate executives, attorneys, and cabinet level official around the globe.

Various international bodies such as the United Nations (ICTY) and NATO H.Q. Brussels, as well as governments such as the former Soviet Union, The Netherlands, Lithuania, Uzbekistan, Sri Lanka, the Sultanate of Oman, Ukraine and Austrian Government have utilized the services and methodology of the Goodfield Institute and the Goodfield Foundation.

Dr. Goodfield is a member of the following organizations:
- Diplomat, American Board of Forensic Examiners
- Diplomat, American Board of Forensic Medicine
- Diplomat, American Board of Psychology Specialists, Clinical Psychology
- Diplomat, American Academy of Experts in Traumatic Stress
- Diplomat, National Center for Crisis Management
- Member, American Psychological Association
- Member, American Federation of Television and Radio Artists
- Member, California Association of Marriage and Family Therapist
- Member, International Society of Police Surgeons, Inc.
- Member, Parliamentarians Network for Conflict Prevention
- Member, Phoenix Committee on Foreign Relations

Websites
www.goodfieldinstitute.com
www.goodfieldinstituut.nl
www.goodfieldmediagroup.com
http://on.fb.me/ub26Qa

Dr. Goodfield's YouTube Channel
http://goo.gl/eAew8

*Diplomate, American Board of Forensic Medicine

www.ingramcontent.com/pod-product-compliance
Lightning Source LLC
Chambersburg PA
CBHW040127270326
41927CB00001B/20